MILLARD FILLMORE

ENCYCLOPEDIA of PRESIDENTS

Millard Fillmore

Thirteenth President of the United States

By Jane Clark Casey

Consultant: Charles Abele, Ph.D.
Social Studies Instructor
Chicago Public School System

 CHILDRENS PRESS ®

CHICAGO

First Lady
Abigail Powers Fillmore

To my father: the best teacher I've ever had, the best student I've ever known.

Library of Congress Cataloging-in-Publication Data

Casey, Jane Clark.
  Millard Fillmore / by Jane Clark Casey.
    p.   cm. — (Encyclopedia of presidents)
  Includes index.
  Summary: Examines the life of the president who helped postpone the Civil War with the Compromise of 1850 and who was considered to have destroyed his political career in order to preserve the Union.
  ISBN 0-516-01353-X
  1. Fillmore, Millard, 1800-1874—Juvenile literature. 2. Presidents—United States—Biography—Juvenile literature. [1. Fillmore, Millard, 1800-1874. 2. Presidents.] I. Title. II. Series.
E427.C37
973.6'4'0924—dc19   87-35183
[B]   CIP
[92]   AC

Childrens Press®, Chicago
Copyright ©1988 by Regensteiner Publishing Enterprises, Inc. All rights reserved. Published simultaneously in Canada. Printed in the United States of America.
            8 9 10 R 97 96 95

Picture Acknowledgments

Joseph E. Barrett, Courtesy U.S. Capitol Historical Society—11 (top)

The Bettmann Archive—36, 40, 46, 64 (2 pictures), 68, 86

Historical Pictures Service, Chicago—6, 11 (bottom), 13, 15, 16, 18, 19, 21, 22, 25, 26, 27, 28, 30, 33, 34, 39 (2 pictures), 41, 42, 43, 48, 49, 51, 53, 54, 55, 58, 61, 65 (top left), 66, 69 (2 pictures), 71, 75 (top), 78, 83 (2 pictures), 84, 89

Courtesy Library of Congress—4, 5, 14, 32, 45, 74, 75 (bottom), 76, 77, 80, 88

The Metropolitan Museum of Art, Bequest of Charles Allen Munn—44

National Archives—8

National Portrait Gallery, Smithsonian Institution—50, 56, 57

North Wind Picture Archives—81

Sophia Smith Collection, Smith College, Northampton, MA—65 (top right, bottom left and right)

Courtesy U.S. Bureau of Printing and Engraving—2

Cover design and illustration by Steven Gaston Dobson

The city of Washington, D.C., in 1800

Table of Contents

Millard Fillmore

Chapter 1

The Forgotten President

It was 1865 and the nation was in mourning for the slain president Abraham Lincoln. Tired from a trip and shocked at Lincoln's murder, Millard Fillmore rounded the corner onto Niagara Square in Buffalo, New York. There he found that his majestic home had been smeared with ink because it was not yet draped with purple in honor of the fallen president.

For his strong opposition to the Republican party, Fillmore had been attacked in newspapers throughout the country, rejected by many who once admired him, and called a traitor to the Union. Though proud and active until his death, he died the object of ridicule and hatred. Even to this day, he is the forgotten president. Most Americans know nothing about him except his name.

Millard Fillmore was a self-made man who rose to the presidency of the United States. He was an ambitious man who worked hard at every job he ever held, yet he chose to leave public office four times during his life. Born in 1800, at a time when about one in every seven people in the country was a slave, he was opposed to slavery. Yet those who wanted to end slavery came to hate him. He was a courageous man. Once while he was president, he left the White House to help fight a fire burning fiercely in the Library of Congress. He did not move when an angry senator waved a gun at him during a heated debate.

But some say the story of Millard Fillmore is a story of political courage—a story of his devotion to the Union and how that devotion cost him his place in history.

The log cabin where Millard Fillmore was born in Cayuga County, New York

Chapter 2

A Boy with Big Dreams

Millard Fillmore was born in 1800, the year the United States capital was moved from Philadelphia to Washington, D.C. It was the year Thomas Jefferson was elected president, a time when cotton was the country's most important export. John Chapman, better known as "Johnny Appleseed," was wandering through pioneer settlements in the Ohio Valley, handing out religious pamphlets and apple seeds. It was also a time when children of educated parents were being taught Latin from childhood. But the future president had no such advantages.

Millard was born on January 7 in a log cabin in Cayuga County, New York, separated from the nearest neighbors by four miles of forest and underbrush. He was the second of Nathaniel and Phoebe Fillmore's nine children. Though his parents were uneducated, his ancestors were surely brave and ambitious. His great-grandfather had risked his life to lead an escape from pirates who captured his fishing boat. His grandfather had fought in both the French and Indian War and the American Revolution. His father, though a failure as a farmer, was a hard-working man who warned that "No man ever prospered from wasting his time in sporting." It was a lesson Millard took to heart.

The Fillmores had no money and little time to spare for education. When Millard was just fourteen, he was apprenticed to a cloth maker in Sparta, New York, one hundred miles from his home. Apprenticeship was little different from slavery except that it lasted for only a few years. Millard was bound by an agreement to stay with his master while learning the trade of cloth making. The man was a harsh master whom Millard grew to hate. He once attempted to strike the young apprentice, but Millard said hotly that he would kill the man before taking a beating. In the end, the boy paid his master a small sum for his freedom and walked the hundred miles home.

Millard's experience as an apprentice made a lasting impression. Many years later, he wrote: "It made me feel for the weak and unprotected, and to hate the insolent tyrant in every station of life."

Millard's father quickly arranged another apprenticeship, this time at a mill where wool was carded (untangled) and cloth prepared. At this job, Millard flourished and won the respect of his master, who called him the best apprentice and best workman he had ever had.

Though the entire family library at home had consisted of a Bible, a hymn book, and an almanac, Millard loved reading. He took every opportunity to learn. One of his jobs at the mill was to work the carding machine. That required walking a short distance every two minutes to get a new roll for the machine. Millard opened a dictionary on a desk he had to pass and would read a bit of it each time. He was eager to improve himself and to achieve a higher position in life than the one to which he was born.

Above: Philadelphia wharf in 1800, when the U.S. capital was moving from Philadelphia to Washington, D.C.   Below: A New England cloth mill in the 1820s

Millard also belonged to a library. At that time, this meant that he paid for the opportunity to read books that were passed among the members. When the mill was shut down during slow seasons, he went to a nearby school.

In 1819, Millard decided he was ready to make use of his new learning. Although he had two more years to serve on his apprenticeship, he had saved the thirty dollars needed to buy his freedom. He shocked his master by announcing that he planned to study law instead of pursuing the trade he had learned.

Though most people now think of law as a secure and profitable profession, it was not a safe career for a poor and uneducated young man in those days. There were few law schools. Instead, those who wanted to learn law studied, or "read," with practicing lawyers.

Millard first studied with a county judge near his father's home in Cayuga County but left after a dispute. For a while, it looked as though his legal career might never begin. When his family moved to East Aurora, New York, Millard took a teaching job in nearby Buffalo, which was a thriving, growing city. Eventually he was able to get a job as a clerk at a Buffalo law firm. Though he kept teaching during the school year, he devoted all his free time to learning the law. In 1823, after just one year of clerkship, he was admitted to the practice of law in New York State.

Millard decided to practice law in East Aurora rather than in Buffalo. He knew that, in the smaller town, he would be the only lawyer. Modest about his abilities, he wanted to test them where the competition was limited.

Abigail Powers Fillmore

At the school he had attended during slow times at the mill, Millard had had a teacher named Abigail Powers, the woman who was to become his wife. She was an intelligent, well-read woman and an accomplished musician who shared Millard's love of books. Abigail became his best friend and confidant. He commented later in life that he had never taken any important step without her advice. He would have liked to marry Abigail in 1823, when he moved to East Aurora. Instead, he waited three years until he had built up a successful law practice with many clients. In 1826, he sent for Abigail and they were married.

The village of Ithaca in central New York State in the 1830s

Fillmore held his first public office—recorder of
deeds—in East Aurora. Longing for greater things,
however, he soon returned to Buffalo. There he established a law firm in partnership with Nathan Hall in 1830.
The firm rapidly became one of the most successful in
western New York. Hall and Fillmore formed personal and
professional ties that would last the rest of their lives.
Millard and Abigail soon became active in community
affairs. They campaigned for public education and helped
establish the first public library in Buffalo.

City Hall in New York City in the nineteenth century

People who watched Fillmore work as a lawyer saw in him the same qualities that marked his political career. He did not have the quickness or brilliance of the famous lawyers of his day. Neither was he smooth or eloquent. Instead, he was organized and persistent. His arguments were so methodical that any conclusion he drew seemed to be the only reasonable one. Someone who watched him said:

> In cases of defense, he would discover the main cord of hope whereon the prosecutor depended for the conviction of his client, and with ease he would untwist it, and separating it fibre from fibre, he would leave his client free from its meshes.

15

A portrait of Fillmore from *Gleason's Pictorial Drawing Room Companion*

Chapter 3

Champion of the Weak and Unprotected

By the time he started his law practice in Buffalo, Fillmore had already become a leader in a political party known as the Anti-Masons. At that time, many people feared a group called the Ancient Order of Masons. It was a secret society that did not let just anyone in and made members promise never to reveal what went on at meetings.

Fear of the Masons (also called Freemasons) was especially strong in western New York. A man named William Morgan had disappeared there after writing a book he said revealed the secrets of the Masonic order. The Masons not only refused to help with the search but made fun of those who did. Many people began to believe that Masons were murderers who considered themselves above the law. Among other things, the Anti-Masons wanted to make it illegal for a Mason to hold public office.

Thurlow Weed, political leader and newspaper editor

It is not entirely clear what drew Fillmore to the leadership of the Anti-Masons. Some think he was merely trying to organize a group of supporters around the popular issue of the day. However, Fillmore had an intense belief in living by the law. He surely must have been outraged at the thought of any group that did not feel itself bound by legal limits. Whatever his motive, Fillmore became an ally of Thurlow Weed, an Anti-Masonic leader who published the Rochester *Anti-Masonic Enquirer*. It was the beginning of a lifelong relationship between the two—one that started out in friendship and ended in bitter hatred.

John Quincy Adams,
president from 1825 to 1829

Weed was a political power broker. That is, he liked to
have a group of supporters whom he could direct to vote
for candidates of his choice. He hoped to get New York's
Anti-Masons to support John Quincy Adams's reelection as
president. Adams would be running against Andrew
Jackson.

At their 1828 convention, the National Republicans of
Erie County, New York, came out in favor of Adams, although Jackson eventually won the presidency. They also
selected Fillmore for New York State assemblyman. In a
year when virtually every election in New York was won
by Jackson supporters, Fillmore not only won, but he received more votes than any other candidate in Erie County.

In those days, state assemblymen were elected for one-year terms. Fillmore did relatively little during his first term in 1829 but quickly grew more ambitious and outspoken after his reelection to the 1830 session. Remembering the "insolent tyrant" to whom he had been apprenticed, he set out to help the "weak and unprotected."

In New York, people were sent to prison simply because they could not pay their debts. Fillmore and others argued that this did no good to anyone, since prisoners were not able to earn the money to pay what they owed. In 1830 he submitted a bill to abolish imprisonment for debt, but it failed. He submitted it again in the 1831 session and it finally passed, ending the dreadful practice of imprisonment for debt in New York.

Like many people of his time, Fillmore believed deeply that the "weak and unprotected" could prosper only if commerce prospered. That meant goods had to be bought, sold, and transported on a large scale. His second term in the state assembly gave him a chance to advance one of his lifelong interests: improved means of transporting goods. He began to urge the building of branch canals from the main line of the Erie Canal. From that time on, Fillmore worked to strengthen commerce, trusting that commerce would improve the lot of the common citizen.

He was also concerned that religion not have too great an influence on government. He opposed the New York law that required witnesses to swear they believed in God before they could testify. By that law, he felt, the state was requiring certain religious beliefs. He introduced the bill that abolished this requirement in New York.

A moonlit scene along the Erie Canal

Fillmore's style as a legislator was much like his style as a lawyer. He was direct and spoke only when an argument or explanation seemed absolutely necessary. When he did speak, as one writer of the time put it, "he spoke with mathematical directness. If he did not convince, he left no rankling wound." This ability to pursue a point without offending his opponents was perhaps Fillmore's greatest asset as a leader. He was a peacemaker all his life. People who knew him as a child recalled his settling a dispute at a teenage party by reasoning with the opponents.

Fillmore served his home district well during his three terms as state assemblyman. If his habit of speaking only when it really mattered was unusual, something he did in the fall of 1831 was even more unusual: he chose not to stand for reelection and returned to private life.

Engd by W. J. Edwards.

from Dag. by Brady.

WASHING FOR GOLD IN CALIFORNIA.

Chapter 4

From Anti-Mason to Whig

Though Fillmore returned to private life in 1831, he did not lose his interest in public affairs. By 1832, he and Abigail had become active in the civic and social life of Buffalo. In a simple, two-story house on Franklin Street, near Lake Erie, they entertained with formal dinners. They attended chamber music recitals, dances, and the lectures of traveling speakers. Both avid readers, they supported the public library they had helped establish, giving not only time and money but also books from their own collection. Their private library was remarkable, eventually growing to some four thousand volumes.

It was also during these early years in Buffalo that Fillmore joined the Unitarian Church. He became a lifelong supporter of its goals. He helped draw up the city charter of Buffalo and helped organize and fund the city's first fire-fighting system. He continued to campaign for improvements to the Erie Canal and the harbor at Buffalo, joining with other citizens to badger the New York Canal Commission about their lack of progress.

Opposite page: An engraving of Fillmore, after a daguerreotype by Mathew Brady

23

Fillmore had continued to practice law during his years as a legislator, since state assemblyman was not a full-time job. He had many student law clerks and treated them the way he had wanted his masters to treat him: teaching them patiently, introducing them to people who could help them in their careers, and supporting them financially.

At home, he and Abigail enjoyed and educated their two children—Millard Powers, who was born in 1827, and Mary Abigail, who was born in 1832.

By the time Fillmore left the state assembly, the leaders of Anti-Masonry had seen that their party could not survive as long as it depended on the one issue of Anti-Masonry. There had been no great public uprising against the Masons, and besides, both President Andrew Jackson and his principal rival, Henry Clay, were Masons themselves. Leaving the state assembly gave Fillmore time to reorganize his supporters in western New York. He was elected to the United States Congress as an Anti-Mason in 1832, but by then he was already actively encouraging his supporters to disband the Anti-Masonic party.

When he could not persuade a hardy group of believers in his own district to give up the name Anti-Mason, he resigned from the party, refused to let the Anti-Masons use his name any longer, and openly joined a party that became known as the Whigs. What united the Whigs was their opposition to Andrew Jackson. Whigs shared Fillmore's belief that commerce and manufacturing led to a better life for all Americans. Their strongest support came from financial and industrial sectors. By 1834, Whigs had won control of the New York city council.

This woodcut from the *Anti-Masonic Almanac* of 1833 shows the
alleged abduction of William Morgan by the Masons in 1826.

President Martin Van Buren

In 1836, Fillmore ran for Congress as a Whig and won. Around the country, however, Whigs were backing three different presidential candidates. With the Whig vote split three ways, it was not surprising that the Democrats again elected the president—this time, Martin Van Buren. Fillmore detested Van Buren, whom he blamed for a widespread depression that began in 1837. In Congress, Fillmore opposed the president, especially when it came to banking. Fillmore wanted a system of "free banking," in which state banks operated independently and without federal controls. That system, he was convinced, was better for commerce and industry. Van Buren, however,

William Henry Seward

feared that banks would collapse without federal controls. He supported regulations that he felt would protect the government from the effects of these collapses.

The economic depression strengthened the Whigs, who won major offices in many states in 1838. In New York, William Henry Seward, a Whig, was elected governor. Seward chose Thurlow Weed, who had helped organize his election, to hand out government jobs to loyal Whig supporters—a practice known as "patronage." Whigs also won many more seats in the U.S. House of Representatives that year. Among them was Fillmore, who returned to Washington for his third term as a congressman.

A cartoon showing the U.S. giving Britain the choice of war or peace before the Webster-Ashburton Treaty of 1842. The agreement included an apology for the destruction of the American ship *Caroline* by the British navy.

Chapter 5

A Skilled Legislator

Fillmore had been quiet during his first term in Congress, just as he had been in his first term in the state assembly. He began making a name for himself, however, when he returned in 1837 as a Whig. That year, a rebellion against Great Britain was going on in Canada, which was still a British colony. Though the United States did not take sides, some Americans who lived along the Canadian border were helping the rebels. In December of 1837, British forces attacked and burned the American ship *Caroline* in United States waters. They believed that the *Caroline* was smuggling arms to the insurgents. There was an immediate uproar in the United States. Reaction was particularly strong in Fillmore's district, which bordered Lake Erie, where the attack had occurred.

Throughout his public life, Fillmore had worked for better protection of the harbors and seaways in his area. However, he did not jump into the midst of those who wanted Congress to denounce Great Britain. When a congressional committee drew up an outraged report on the situation, Fillmore argued against it. He had been trying for years to convince the administration to station more troops on the northern borders. Now the committee was trying to substitute angry words for a strong defense.

The British attack on the _Caroline_, December 28, 1832

"I would submit," he argued, "that the best way to avoid a war with Great Britain is to show her that we are prepared to meet her, if there is to be a war; because reasonable preparations for defense are better than gasconading [boasting]." Fillmore believed that being well prepared was more important than spouting big words.

Now in his third term, however, Fillmore gave perhaps the most important and eloquent speech of his congressional career. After the 1838 election, a dispute arose over the elections of five congressmen from New Jersey. The outcome would determine whether the Democrats or the Whigs had a majority in the House of Representatives. That, in turn, would determine who controlled the committees and the passing of laws. So the outcome of the dispute was very important. Although a committee was appointed to investigate these elections, the Democrats managed to stand in its way. They forced the seating of Democratic congressmen in all five seats.

Fillmore was outraged by the Democrats' tricks and attempted to read a minority report (that is, a report describing the Whigs' side of the dispute) in the House. The Democratic Speaker of the House would not allow it. He claimed that Fillmore needed permission of the House to present such a report, while Fillmore believed that he had an absolute right to do so. Furious that the majority was unwilling even to listen to the comments of the minority, Fillmore gave one of the few passionate speeches of his career. He warned that the majority was acting dangerously in silencing the minority, since the same rule could be used against them someday. He said:

> The majority possesses all the power; the minority have nothing to protect them but the Constitution and the rules of the House; and if these are broken, then farewell to freedom, farewell to all that is dear to an American citizen! This hall becomes the temple of despotism [rule by a tyrant], and you, Mr. Speaker, its highest priest.

The usually reserved congressman had, as ever, "hated the insolent tyrant" and spoken out against him.

31

Daniel Webster

By 1840, the Whigs had finally become organized nationally. A Whig, William Henry Harrison, was elected president, and Whigs controlled both houses of Congress. For the first time in his career, Fillmore was a member of the ruling party. Two famous American statesmen, Henry Clay and Daniel Webster, were competing for control of the Whigs. Most Whig leaders expected President Harrison, an aging war hero, to serve as a figurehead—that is, to be a symbol of their cause but not its real leader. It was Clay and Webster who fought for actual control over the party. This was an important struggle, since whoever controlled the Whig party controlled the United States government. Had Harrison remained president, one of these two would probably have won the struggle within the Whig party and made most of the important decisions of Harrison's presidency.

William Henry Harrison

In an unexpected turn of events, Harrison became ill and died within a few weeks of taking office. His vice-president, John Tyler, became president. Although he ran as a Whig, Tyler was really a Democrat and was at odds with the Whigs on several important issues. Among these was the question of a privately owned national bank. Fillmore and other Whigs favored such a bank, but Tyler opposed it. Four years of bickering took place between him and the Whigs who controlled Congress. At one point, Clay and his friends managed to pass a bill creating a privately owned national bank, only to have Tyler veto it. Fillmore and Webster tried to get Tyler to sign a compromise bill but the president refused. Having already offended Clay and his supporters by vetoing Clay's bill, Tyler was now cut off from Webster and his supporters as well. He was a president without a party.

President John Tyler

During this period, there was an ongoing battle over tariffs, the taxes placed on imported goods. On one side were the free traders, who wanted tariffs to be eliminated or at least made very low. On the other side were the protectionists, who favored high tariffs. The free traders were mostly those who produced raw goods, such as farm products, and the protectionists were mostly manufacturers. In the United States, this meant that free traders tended to be southerners, while protectionists tended to be northeasterners.

Fillmore, as the champion of industrial interests in the House, was naturally a protectionist. Selected chairman of the powerful House Ways and Means Committee in 1841, he devoted himself to preserving the high tariffs that were in effect then. At the same time, he hoped to keep President Tyler in political trouble, since he believed that Tyler had betrayed the Whigs who had put him in office. Fillmore accomplished both goals with great political skill.

With no federal income tax in those days, the federal government got its income from sources such as tariffs and the sale of public lands. Fillmore proposed that money from land sales be given to the states instead. Then the government would depend on high tariffs even more for its income. He introduced several bills that were strongly backed by the Whigs but opposed by southern Democrats. When Tyler vetoed them, Whigs were so enraged that they called for his impeachment, or removal from office.

Fillmore then delayed both the tariff and the land sale issues in his committee until June 1842, only a month before the tariffs were set to expire. By that time, the federal government was desperate for money. Fillmore then supported another bill. This one dropped the requirement that land sale proceeds go to the states, but *increased* tariffs by about 30 percent. Tyler was forced to sign this bill in order to have funds to run the government. Fillmore became the hero of protectionists everywhere and earned new respect for the skill he had shown in meeting his two goals. The high tariffs were still in place, and Tyler had no supporters left.

Despite his newfound fame, Fillmore chose not to run for Congress again in 1842. He had had enough of serving under Tyler. He turned his attention to his political organization in New York, which badly needed his leadership.

Millard Fillmore

Chapter 6

Tending the Home Fires

Fillmore's Whig party in New York was being torn apart by a number of forces. People were frightened by the tremendous increase in immigration, and a strong anti-immigrant feeling was growing in parts of New York. Between 1830 and 1840 alone, about 600,000 immigrants had arrived in the United States. These immigrants, largely European, tended to live in the industrial areas of the East.

Many people, including Fillmore, were afraid that these new arrivals might not understand and appreciate the democratic way of life that earlier Americans had fought for. People also feared the voting power of these immigrants, who were largely Roman Catholic. They thought that the Pope, the leader of the church in Rome, Italy, would control the immigrants' votes. (While this attitude may seem surprising, it should be noted that many people opposed the candidacy of John F. Kennedy in 1960 for the same reason!)

Around 1842, some Whigs in New York banded together with a group called "nativists," who were organized around protecting "native" interests against this increasing group of Catholic European immigrants. This group called itself the American Republican party and was especially active in New York City.

At the same time, abolitionist forces were growing and becoming a real political power. The American Anti-Slavery Society, founded in 1833 by abolitionists in New York and New England, was growing, particularly in western New York. By 1834, the abolitionists had caused enough stir to provoke an *anti*-abolition riot in New York City.

In 1838, the first of the northern states' "personal liberty laws" was passed. These were laws that interfered with the national Fugitive Slave Act, which required the return of runaway slaves. A system of escape routes known as the Underground Railroad had been developed to help slaves get out of the South, and tension was rising over the question of their owners' right to their return. Slave owners wanted strict enforcement of the act, while abolitionists did everything they could to interfere with its enforcement. In 1839, the first antislavery party, known as the Liberty party, held its national convention in Warsaw, New York, not far from Fillmore's home.

Fillmore had been personally and publicly opposed to slavery since at least 1835, when he first spoke out on the question. On this occasion he presented a petition to the House of Representatives from the people of Rochester, New York, urging that slavery be abolished in the nation's capital of Washington, D.C. (There was a flourishing slave market in that city, visible from the Capitol building.) However, Congress at that time simply "tabled" all petitions on the subject; that is, they took no action on them. Fillmore also opposed the annexation of Texas so long as it was a slave state and favored attempts by Congress to help eliminate the slave trade altogether.

Above: William Lloyd Garrison, a founder of the American Anti-Slavery Society, in the hands of a Boston anti-abolitionist mob in 1835.   Below: Garrison with fellow abolitionists George Thompson (left) and Wendell Phillips (right)

TO BE SOLD, on board the Ship *Bance-Island*, on tuesday the 6th of *May* next, at *Ashley Ferry*; a choice cargo of about 250 fine healthy NEGROES, just arrived from the Windward & Rice Coast. —The utmost care has already been taken, and shall be continued, to keep them free from the least danger of being infected with the SMALL-POX, no boat having been on board, and all other communication with people from *Charles-Town* prevented.

Austin, Laurens, & Appleby.

N. B. Full one Half of the above Negroes have had the SMALL-POX in their own Country.

Announcement for a slave sale in Charleston, South Carolina

He would not, however, pledge support for any particular measure. "If I stand pledged to a particular course of action," he said, "I cease to be a responsible agent [of the voters], but I become a mere machine." Was he trying to get out of taking sides on a touchy issue? More likely, he understood that the dispute over slavery would not be resolved through any simple means. He saw that the compromises necessary to eliminate the slave trade peacefully would be very complicated.

A Whig parade in New York City during the 1844 presidential campaign

With the nativists and the abolitionists assembling in New York, Fillmore had his hands full trying to keep his political organization together. In 1841 Whigs had lost a number of seats in the state assembly, partly because Tyler was an unpopular president, but more so because the Whig governor, William Seward, had offended many voters. From 1842 to 1844, Fillmore devoted himself to private law practice, enjoyed having a comfortable income for the first time in his life, and managed to maintain control of the local Whig organization. He began to think about running for vice-president in 1844.

Henry Clay

Thurlow Weed, desperate to retain his Whig stronghold in New York, had other plans for Fillmore. At the 1844 Whig convention, he blocked Fillmore's nomination as Henry Clay's vice-presidential running mate. Instead, he had Fillmore nominated for governor of New York.

Fillmore did not want to run for governor—nor did he trust Weed. He may have foreseen a disaster for the Whigs that year. If so, he was right. The enormous immigrant population in New York City voted overwhelmingly against Whig candidates. They identified the Whigs with the anti-immigrant nativists. Abolitionists, who saw Henry Clay as a proslavery candidate, voted against the entire Whig ticket. The Whigs were beaten so badly that Fillmore won in his own ward by only four votes. It was the first political defeat of his career, and he held it against the urban immigrants for the rest of his life.

Millard Fillmore's home in Buffalo, New York

For several years, Fillmore lived quietly in Buffalo, practicing law, teaching his son, Powers, how to be a lawyer, and remaining active in local civic affairs. He watched the new president, James K. Polk, with dismay, and began to view Polk's election as a disaster for the country. The high tariff Fillmore had so skillfully protected in 1842 was lifted. Banking measures he had successfully defeated were brought back and passed. The war with Mexico continued to drain American funds and cost American lives. Fillmore saw that war as an outrage to the North. He felt it was creating a huge national debt only to bring another slave territory under United States control. Finally, although commerce was growing rapidly in the Great Lakes states, Polk vetoed an 1846 bill to improve the rivers and harbors there.

Broadway and City Hall in New York City in the 1820s

Fillmore's rift with Thurlow Weed was widening. In the 1846 race for New York governor, Fillmore backed John Young instead of Weed's candidate, Ira Harris. Young won, and Weed's control of the New York Whig party was damaged. Like Fillmore, Weed had a long memory. His list of complaints against Fillmore was growing.

In 1847, Weed and Fillmore patched their differences briefly, and Fillmore ran for comptroller of New York State. This was a major office wielding about as much power as the governor. After winning with the largest vote

Fillmore's wife, Abigail

ever amassed by a Whig candidate in New York, Fillmore sold his law books, moved his wife to Albany, and settled in to the full-time work of his new position. He sent Powers off to Harvard and his daughter, Mary Abigail, to a finishing school in Massachusetts. Although Fillmore served only one year as comptroller, he was able to improve and enlarge canals during that time. In addition, the state assembly adopted his proposal for a banking code revision. And the currency system he proposed in it was adopted sixteen years later as the National Banking Act.

Chapter 7

Vice-President under a Threat to the Union

As the Whigs approached the 1848 presidential election, they knew they needed the support of their southern allies. Southern Whigs, who tended to be the largest plantation owners and hence the largest slaveholders, knew that Whigs and abolitionists were working together in the North. Southerners were determined that the Whig nomination should go to a southern candidate that year. The man they wanted was Zachary Taylor, a sugar planter and slaveholder who had served as a general in the war with Mexico. Competing with Taylor for the Whig nomination was Henry Clay, who supported high tariffs and was seen by southerners as an antislavery candidate. Feelings ran high and the race was close, but Taylor won the nomination on the fourth ballot. When he did, one strong antislavery delegate jumped up onto a table and announced that the selection of Taylor marked the end of the Whig party.

An 1861 photograph of Thurlow Weed

At that moment, a New York delegate named John Collier rose. He said that he was a Clay supporter and opposed slavery, but that he would support Taylor. He proposed a vice-presidential candidate who could heal the rift between the slavery and antislavery delegates: Millard Fillmore. Collier gave the impression that Fillmore was a Clay supporter (which he was not) and that he was strongly opposed to slavery (which was not entirely accurate). Nevertheless, the mood of the moment was such that Fillmore was nominated on only the second vote. Fillmore's victory naturally raised his own standing within the party. What is more, it thwarted the plans of Thurlow Weed. Weed had publicly backed a wealthy New England merchant named Abbott Lawrence but privately hoped to arrange the nomination of his favorite, William Seward. This was simply one more item in the long list of grievances that were driving Weed and Fillmore apart.

Zachary Taylor

During his campaign for the vice-presidency, Fillmore quickly made it clear that he would not encourage the federal government to take an active role in opposing slavery. He had always "regarded slavery as an evil, but one with which the National Government had nothing to do." By that, he meant that the Constitution allowed individual states to decide whether to permit or ban slavery; he believed that the federal government had no right to interfere. He took no position on the issue of slavery in the territories (lands controlled by the United States, but not yet admitted as states).

Taylor and Fillmore were narrowly elected, and Fillmore set out for Washington. Sadly, he was not accompanied by Abigail, whose health and spirits had declined so badly that she chose to stay in Buffalo. She wrote him daily, however, and he visited as often as he could, relying as always on her advice.

The United States Senate chamber in 1850

As vice-president, Fillmore would preside over the Senate. He was, according to custom, sworn in in the Senate chamber. In those days, the room was heated with grate fires burning hickory wood. Members gathered round the fires to stay warm or wrapped themselves in long woolen scarves at their desks. Fillmore was naturally conservative and must have felt at home among these men in somber suits and tall silk hats. He did not, however, keep wine on his desk, as many of the members did. Fillmore never drank.

As soon as they got into office, Taylor and his supporters began trying to calm the northern Whigs who had feared Taylor's southern ties. Taylor's men ignored Fillmore and dealt directly with Thurlow Weed, who was

General Winfield Scott
entering Mexico City
after his victory there

attempting to gain control over all the federal jobs in New York. Weed fired and replaced Fillmore's people and ignored his recommendations on hiring. He attacked Fillmore openly in his publications and, by December 1849, had destroyed Fillmore's political organization in New York.

President Taylor, meanwhile, was wondering what to do with the new lands acquired from Mexico. The Treaty of Guadalupe Hidalgo, which ended the Mexican War in 1848, gave the United States control over the area that is now California, Nevada, Utah, New Mexico, and Arizona. Residents of those areas were already asking for statehood. This was a very controversial topic.

The Senate was evenly divided between slave and free states. To admit even one more state in either group would tip the balance. Senator William Seward, who was backed by Weed, proposed that the new land be brought in as states rather than territories. That way, each new state, and not Congress, would decide whether slavery would be allowed. Whigs and southern Democrats strongly opposed this measure, but President Taylor favored it.

In a message to Congress in 1850, Taylor proposed that California and New Mexico be admitted as states and allowed to decide their own status—slave or free. Since California had just adopted a constitution banning slavery, Taylor's plan had no chance of getting through a proslavery Democratic Congress. His proposal also angered southerners, who viewed it as an insult. Southern leaders began to talk about breaking with the Union, or seceding. Their idea was to dissolve the Union and allow the South to become its own country—a country in which slavery was tolerated. Northerners were opposed to secession. It would have robbed them of their trade with the South and virtually guaranteed that slavery continue.

Political leaders began to seek a compromise that could hold the Union together. In January 1850, Henry Clay proposed one scheme: (1) admit California as a free state; (2) divide New Mexico into two territories that would decide their free or slave status after they became states; (3) abolish the slave trade in the nation's capital; and (4) enforce a much tougher Fugitive Slave Act.

Senator Stephen A. Douglas, a Democrat from Illinois, proposed a different version. His plan called for the two

Stephen A. Douglas

New Mexico territories (eventually, New Mexico and Utah) to vote slave or free before being admitted as states. William Seward, who saw the Fugitive Slave Law as "a pact with the devil," suggested that the North secede if an agreement to enforce it passed. Taylor, relying on Seward, opposed a compromise.

But New York merchants began pushing for Clay's compromise. Fillmore supported that drive, but he did so privately. He was still trying to get back into the good graces of the president to regain control of federal jobs in New York. Debate on what became known as the Compromise of 1850 continued.

Senator Daniel Webster

Senator Daniel Webster, one of the most famous statesmen of the century, rose to speak in favor of the compromise. His comments have come to be known as his "Seventh of March" speech. He said that, according to the Supreme Court, the federal government was responsible for the return of runaway slaves. He went on:

> What right have they [the abolitionists in Congress] in their legislative capacity or any capacity, to endeavor to get round this Constitution, or to embarrass the free exercise of the rights secured by the Constitution to persons whose slaves escape from them? None at all; none at all. Neither in the forum of conscience, nor before the face of the Constitution, are they, in my opinion, justified in such an attempt.

VOTERS, Read This!

EXTRACT FROM A

SPEECH

DELIVERED BY THE

Hon. Daniel Webster,

IN THE SENATE OF THE UNITED STATES,
ON THE 7th OF MARCH, 1850.

"If the infernal Fanatics and Abolitionists ever get the power in their hands, they will override the Constitution, set the Supreme Court at defiance, change and make Laws to suit themselves. They will lay violent hands on those who differ with them politically in opinion, or dare question their infallibility; bankrupt the country and finally deluge it with blood."

A handbill on Webster's "Seventh of March" speech

For Webster, this speech was an act of courage. It angered his northern supporters and cost him his dream of becoming president someday himself. Eventually, though, he was persuaded that preservation of the Union demanded a compromise that would appease the South.

Senator Jefferson Davis

As debate on the compromise dragged on into the summer, congressional tempers began to match the hot, humid weather. At one point, Senator Henry Foote of Mississippi entered the chamber waving a revolver. While others scrambled to get out of the way, Fillmore drew himself up in the presiding officer's chair and called for order until Foote was restrained. Senator Robert Barnwell of South Carolina warned in July that if the North claimed the right to interfere with slavery in the South, then the South would seek independence. The next day, Senator Robert Hunter of Virginia said that passage of the compromise would "open the gates of war." Senator Jefferson Davis of Mississippi, who would go on to head the Confederate

Henry Clay speaking in the Senate chamber, with Fillmore presiding

States of America during the Civil War, opposed the compromise. He said he did not trust the North to enforce the Fugitive Slave Act (and he was correct). Throughout the South, conventions were being called to discuss secession while southern leaders threatened to make it a reality.

Obviously, if Congress were to vote on a compromise bill, the vote would be close. If there were a tie, Vice-President Fillmore, as president of the Senate, would have to cast the tie-breaking vote—something he did not want to do. He favored the compromise, but to vote in its favor, he knew, would be political suicide. Like Webster, however, he felt that it was more important to preserve the Union than to preserve his own political future.

57

Chapter 8

New Burdens and New Powers

Fillmore never had to cast that dreaded vote. Instead, he inherited an even more sobering responsibility. On July 9, 1850, President Taylor died after a brief illness. Fillmore, who had learned only at noon that day that the president was gravely ill, was alone in Washington. His wife was in Buffalo, and even his daughter, who often stayed with him during his vice-presidency, had left Washington to escape the heat. He locked the door and spent what he described as the only sleepless night he ever had over political issues. He thought of the crisis that faced the Union. He brooded over the unhappy administration of President Tyler, the only other vice-president to succeed to the presidency. In the morning, he was sworn in as president of the United States.

Even before he could deal with the problem of the compromise, he had to find replacements for Taylor's cabinet. Since all its members had sided with Weed to undercut Fillmore's political power, he could not rely on their support. All turned in their resignations, and he set about putting together a group of advisers who shared his belief that any legal course was preferable to civil war.

Despite his strong personal opposition to slavery, he had an even stronger belief in states' rights. The Constitution, he believed, had to be strictly read. He believed that the president had limited powers and that Congress should govern the country, so long as it did not violate the Constitution. He sincerely believed that, according to the Constitution, the individual states had the right to determine whether slavery would be permitted within their borders.

For his cabinet he selected prominent Whig leaders, all of them committed to the compromise. Among them was his former law partner, Nathan Hall, as postmaster general and Senator Daniel Webster as secretary of state.

On July 15, Congress resumed debate on the compromise. Webster, in his last speech as a senator, called for the enactment of all parts of the compromise as one "omnibus" bill. If that were not possible, he asked that each part be enacted separately. At the same time, Fillmore sent word to Congress that he would sign any measure they passed, as long as it was constitutional.

But the omnibus bill failed to make it through the Senate. Instead, individual parts of it were submitted to a vote. On August 9, 1850, the first of the compromise bills passed, resolving the border dispute between Texas and New Mexico. Other bills were approved in rapid order: California was given statehood; Utah and New Mexico were given territorial governments and allowed to decide for themselves whether to permit slavery; the slave trade was abolished in Washington, D.C.; and a stronger Fugitive Slave Act was passed. By mid-September, the House of Representatives had approved these bills as well.

Opposite page: The fugitive slave bill that became part of the Compromise of 1850

Fugitive Slave Bill.

As passed by the Senate and House of Representatives, Sept 12, 1850, and approved September 18, 1850, by President FILLMORE.

AN ACT to amend, and supplementary to the act entitled, "An act respecting fugitives from justice, and persons escaping from the service of their masters," approved, Feb. 12, 1793.

SECTION 1. That persons who have been or may hereafter be, appointed Commissioners in virtue of any act of Congress, by the Circuit Courts of the United States, and who in consequence of such appointments, are authorised to exercise the powers that a *justice of the peace or other magistrate* of any of the United States may exercise in respect to offenders for any crime or offence against the United States, by arresting, imprisoning, or bailing the same under and by virtue of the thirty-third section of the act of the 24th of September, 1789, entitled "An act to establish Judicial Courts of the United States," shall be and are hereby *authorized and required to exercise and discharge all the powers and duties conferred by this act*.

SEC 2. And be it further enacted, That the Superior Court of *each organized territory* of the United States, shall have the same power to appoint commissioners to take acknowledgements of bail and affidavits, and to take depositions of witnesses in civil causes which is now possessed by the Circuit Courts of the United States; all commissioners who shall be appointed for such purposes by the Superior Court of *any organized territory* of the United States, shall possess all the powers and exercise all the duties conferred by law upon the commissioners appointed by the Circuit Court of the United States for similar purposes, and shall moreover exercise and discharge all the powers and duties conferred by this act.

SEC. 3. And be it further enacted, That the circuit courts of the United States and the superior courts of each organized territory of the United States, shall, from time to time, *enlarge the number of commissioners, with a view to afford reasonable facilities to reclaim fugitives from labor*, and to the discharge of the duties imposed by this act.

SEC. 4. And be it further enacted, That the commissioners above named shall have concurrent jurisdiction with the Judges of the Circuit and District Courts of the United States, in their respective circuits and districts within the several States, and the judges of the superior courts of the territories, severally and collectively, in term time and vacation; and shall grant certificates to such claimants, upon *satisfactory proof* being made with *authority to take and remove such fugitives from service or labor*, under the restrictions herein contained, to the State or territory from which such persons may have escaped or fled.

SEC. 5. And be it further enacted, That it shall be the duty of all marshals and deputy marshals to obey and execute all warrants and precepts issued under the provisions of this act, when to them directed; and should any marshal or deputy marshal *refuse* to receive such warrant or other process, when tendered, or use all proper means diligently to execute the same, he shall on conviction thereof, be *fined in the sum of ONE THOUSAND DOLLARS to the use of such claimant* on motion of such claimant, by the circuit or district court of the district of such marshal; and after arrest of such fugitive by such marshal or his deputy, or whilst at any time in his custody under the provisions of this act, should such fugitive escape, *whether* WITH OR WITHOUT THE ASSENT OF SUCH MARSHAL OR HIS DEPUTY, such marshal shall be liable on his official bond to be prosecuted for the benefit of such claimant, for the *full value* of the service or labor of said fugitive in the State, territory or district whence he escaped; and the better to enable the said commissioners when thus appointed, to execute their duties faithfully and efficiently; in conformity with the requirements of the Constitution of the United States and of this act, they are hereby authorized and empowered, *within their counties* respectively to appoint in writing under hands *any one or more suitable persons* from time to time, to execute all such warrants and other process as may be issued by them in the lawful performance of their respective duties, with authority to such commissioners or the person to be appointed by them to execute process as aforesaid, to summon and CALL TO THEIR AID THE BYSTANDERS, or *posse comitatus* of the proper county, when necessary to insure a faithful observance of the clause of the constitution referred to, in conformity with the provisions of this act—AND ALL GOOD CITIZENS ARE HEREBY COMMANDED TO AID AND ASSIST IN THE PROMPT AND EFFICIENT EXECUTION OF THIS WHENEVER THEIR SERVICES MAY BE REQUIRED as aforesaid for that purpose; and said warrants shall run and be executed by said officers anywhere in the State, within which they are executed.

SEC. 6. And be it further enacted, That when a person held to service or labor in any State or territory of the United States, *has heretofore or shall hereafter* escape into another State or territory of the United States, the person or persons to whom such services or labor may be due, or his, her or their agent or attorney, duly authorized, by power of attorney, in writing acknowledged and certified under the seal of some legal officer of court of the State or territory in which the same may be executed, may pursue and reclaim such fugitive person, either by procuring a warrant from some of the courts, judges or commissioners aforesaid, of the proper circuit, district or county for the apprehension of such fugitive from service or labor, or by seizing and arresting such fugitive, where the same can be done *without process*, and by taking or causing such person to be taken, forthwith before such court, judge or commissioner, whose duty it shall be to hear and determine the case of such claimant *in a* SUMMARY MANNER; and upon *satisfactory proof* being made, by *deposition or affidavit*, in writing, to be taken and certified by such court, judge or commissioner, or by *other satisfactory testimony*, duly taken and certified by some court, magistrate, justice of the peace, or other legal officer authorised to administer an oath and take depositions under the laws of the State or territory from which such person owing service or labor may have escaped, with a certificate of such magistracy or other authority, as aforesaid, with the seal of the proper court or officer thereto attached, which seal shall be sufficient to establish the competency of the proof, and with proof also by affidavit, of the *identity* of the person whose service or labor is said to be due as aforesaid, that the person so arrested does in fact owe service or labor to the person or persons claiming him or her, in the State or territory from which such fugitive may have escaped, as aforesaid, and that said person escaped, to make out and deliver to such claimant, his or her agent or attorney, a *certificate* setting forth the substantial facts as to the service or labor due from such fugitive to the claimant, and of his or her escape from the State or territory in which such service or labor was due, to the State or territory in which he or she was arrested, *with authority to such claimant or his or her agent or attorney, to use such reasonable force and restraint as may be necessary*, under the circumstances of the case, to take and remove such fugitive person back to the State or territory from whence he or she may have escaped as aforesaid. IN NO TRIAL OR HEARING UNDER THIS ACT SHALL TESTIMONY OF SUCH ALLEGED FUGITIVE BE ADMITTED IN EVIDENCE; and *the certificates in this and the first section mentioned* SHALL BE CONCLUSIVE OF THE RIGHT OF THE PERSON OR PERSONS IN WHOSE FAVOR GRANTED, *to remove such fugitive to the State or territory from which he escaped, and shall prevent all molestation of said person or persons by any process issued by any court, judge, magistrate or other person whomsoever*.

SEC. 7. And be it further enacted, That any person who shall knowingly or willingly obstruct, hinder or prevent such claimant, his agent or attorney, or *any person or persons*, lawfully assisting him, her or them, from arresting such fugitive from service or labor EITHER WITH *or* WITHOUT PROCESS as aforesaid; or shall rescue, or attempt to rescue such fugitive from service or labor, from the custody of such claimant, his or her agent or attorney, or other person or persons lawfully assisting as aforesaid when so arrested, pursuant to the authority herein given and declared; OR SHALL AID, ABET, OR ASSIST SUCH A PERSON SO OWING SERVICE OR LABOR AS AFORESAID, DIRECTLY OR INDIRECTLY TO ESCAPE from such claimant, his agent or attorney, or other person or persons legally authorized as aforesaid, or SHALL HARBOR or CONCEAL such fugitive, so as to prevent the discovery and arrest of such person, after notice or knowledge of the fact that such person was a fugitive from service or labor as aforesaid, shall, for either of said offences be subject to *a fine not exceeding* ONE THOUSAND DOLLARS *and* IMPRISONMENT NOT EXCEEDING SIX MONTHS, by indictment and conviction before the district court of the United States for the district in which such offence may have been committed, or before the proper court of criminal jurisdiction if committed within any one of the *organized territories* of the United States; *and shall, moreover, forfeit and pay by way of civil damages to the party injured by such illegal conduct, the sum of* ONE THOUSAND DOLLARS FOR EACH FUGITIVE SO LOST, as aforesaid, to be recovered by action for debt, in any of the district or territorial courts aforesaid, within whose jurisdiction the said offence may have been committed.

SEC. 8. And be it further enacted, That the marshals, their deputies, and the clerks of the said district and territorial courts, shall be paid for their services the like fees as may be allowed to them for similar services in other cases; and where such services are rendered exclusively in the arrest, custody and delivery of the fugitive to the claimant, his or her agent or attorney, or where such supposed fugitive may be discharged out of custody for want of sufficient proof as aforesaid, then such fees are to be paid in the whole by such claimant, his agent or attorney; and in all cases where the proceedings are before a commissioner, he shall be entitled to a fee of TEN DOLLARS in full for his services in each case, *upon the delivery of the said certificate to the claimant*, his or her agent or attorney; or a fee of FIVE DOLLARS *in cases where the proof shall not in the opinion of such commissioner, warrant such certificate and delivery*, inclusive of all services incident to such arrest and examination, to be paid, in either case, by the claimant, his or her agent or attorney. The person or persons authorized to execute the process to be issued by such commissioners for the arrest and detention of fugitives from service or labor, as aforesaid, shall also be entitled to a fee of *five dollars each* for said person he or they may arrest and take before any such commissioner as aforesaid, at the instance and request of such claimant, with such other fees as may be deemed reasonable by such commissioner for such additional services as may be necessarily performed by him or them; such as attending at the examination, keeping the fugitive in custody, and providing him with food and lodging during his detention, and until the final determination of such commissioner; and in general for performing such other duties as may be required by such claimant, his or her attorney or agent, or commissioner in the premises, such fees to be made up in conformity with the fees usually charged by the officers of the courts of justice within the proper district or county, as near as may be practicable, and paid by such claimants, their agents or attorneys, whether such supposed fugitives from service or labor, be ordered to be delivered to such claimants by the final determination of such commissioner or not.

SEC. 9. And be it further enacted, That upon affidavit made by the claimant of such fugitive, his agent or attorney, after such certificate has been issued, that he has reason to apprehend that *such fugitive will be rescued by force* from his or their possessions before he can be taken beyond the limits of the State in which the arrest is made, it shall be the duty of the officer making the arrest to *retain the fugitive in his custody, and to remove him to the State whence he fled*, and there to deliver him to said claimant, his agent or attorney. And to this end, the officer aforesaid is hereby AUTHORIZED AND REQUIRED TO EMPLOY SO MANY PERSONS AS HE MAY DEEM NECESSARY to overcome such force, and to retain them in his service so long as circumstances require. The said officer and his assistants, while so employed to receive the same compensation, and to be allowed the same expenses as are now allowed by law for transportation of criminals, to be certified by the judge of the district within which the arrest is made, and PAID OUT OF THE TREASURY OF THE UNITED STATES.

SEC. 10. And be it further enacted, That when any person held to service or labor in any State or Territory, or in the District of Columbia, shall escape therefrom, the party to whom such service or labor shall be due, his, her or their agent or attorney may apply to any court of record therein, or judge thereof in vacation, and make satisfactory proof to such court or judge in vacation, of the escape aforesaid, and that the person escaping owed service or labor to such party. Whereupon the court shall cause a record to be made of the matter as proved, and also a general description of the persons escaping with such convenient certainty as may be, and a transcript of such record authenticated by the attestation of clerk and seal of the said court being produced in any other State, Territory or District in which the person so escaping may be found, and being exhibited to any judge, commissioner or other officer authorized by the law of the United States to cause persons escaping from service or labor to be delivered up, *shall be held and taken to be full and conclusive evidence of escape, and that the service or labor of the person escaping is due to the party in such record mentioned*. And upon the production by the said party of other and further evidence, *if necessary either oral or by affidavit*, in addition to what is contained in the said record of the identity of the person escaping, *he or she shall be up to the claimant*.—And the said court, commissioner, judge or other person authorized by this act to grant certificates to claimants of fugitives, shall upon the production of the record and other evidences aforesaid, grant to such claimant a certificate of his right to take any such person identified and proved to be owing service or labor as aforesaid, which certificate shall authorize such claimaint to seize or arrest and transport such person to the State or Territory from which he escaped. Provided,

That nothing herein contained shall be construed *as requiring the production of a transcript of such record as evidence as aforesaid*. But in its absence the claim shall be heard and determined upon other satisfactory proofs competent in law.

Approved, September 18, 1850.

MILLARD FILLMORE.

THE BLACK LIST.

Total vote from free States in favor of the Fugitive Slave bill

DEMOCRATS —*Maine*—Messrs. Fuller, Gerry, Littlefield—3.

New Hampshire.—Messrs. HIBBARD and PEASLEE—2.

New York—Mr Walden—1.

New Jersey—Mr Wildrick—1.

Pennsylvania—Messrs Dimmick, Job Mann, McLanahan, Robbins, Ross and James Thompson—6.

Ohio—Messrs. Hayland and Miller—2.

Indiana—Messrs, Alberston, William J. Brown, Dunham, Gorman, McDonald—5.

Illinois—Messrs. Bissel, T. L. Harris, McClernand, Richardson, Young—5.

Michigan—Mr A. W. Buel—1.

Iowa—Mr Leffler—1.

California—Mr Gilbert—1. Total 27.

WHIGS.—Messrs. Elliot, of *Mass.*; McGaughey of *Ind.*; John L. Taylor, of *Ohio*—Total, 3

Total Ayes from free states, 30.

The passage of these bills was widely viewed as having ended a real threat of civil war. When House approval was certain, a large crowd gathered in the capital to celebrate. The Marine Band played patriotic tunes and a one-hundred-gun salute was fired. The crowd sang to the president and to Webster and Clay. It was their way of saying "thank you" to these men for preserving the Union.

Once Congress had acted, Fillmore quickly signed all the bills except the Fugitive Slave Act. That law said that slaves were the property of their owners and must be returned, wherever they were found. It was based on a passage in the United States Constitution that required slaves to be delivered up to their owners, even if they were found in a nonslave state.

Thus, a slave who escaped into the North was still not safe. If he or she could be located, the owner could insist that the slave be returned. George Washington had signed the first Fugitive Slave Act in 1793, but it had not been enforced since the early 1840s. State and local officials in the North simply refused to cooperate, and federal officials ignored the law.

The 1850 Fugitive Slave Act was much stronger than the one Washington had signed. It placed enforcement of the law solely in the hands of federal officials. In addition, it provided for a larger number of such officials and gave them greater powers than they had had under the old act.

The concept of treating human beings as property was repugnant to Fillmore. Abigail warned her husband that signing the act would be the end of his political career. But he believed that Congress should make policy for the nation, and he had given his word. With great reluctance, he signed the act into law.

Antislavery campaigners turned their full attention to resisting the new Fugitive Slave Act. The need to enforce it placed it prominently in the public eye.

Abolitionists argued that there was a higher law—a divine law—that made men free. They called on others to resist enforcement of that act through civil disobedience—deliberately refusing to obey the law in order to provoke change.

Whatever Fillmore's personal thoughts may have been, he did not believe that the president should be involved in civil disobedience. He chose to enforce the law. When a mob freed a slave from a jail in Pennsylvania, where he was being held until he could be returned to his master in the South, Fillmore sent federal troops to assist the jailers. He wrote to Daniel Webster:

> God knows I detest slavery, but . . . we must endure it and give it such protection as is guaranteed by the constitution, till we can get rid of it without destroying the last hope of free government in the world.

By approving the Fugitive Slave Act, Fillmore earned the hatred of abolitionists everywhere. Yet he had done what he thought necessary to save the Union without armed conflict.

When his own pastor criticized him for signing the act, Fillmore responded that he had chosen between two evils. One was the temporary evil of allowing slavery to continue until it died on its own. The other evil would be to bring on an era of bloodshed, with the destruction of the country as a probable result.

Above: Poster for a stage presentation of *Uncle Tom's Cabin*
Below: The slave Henry Brown, shipped to Philadelphia and freed by abolitionists

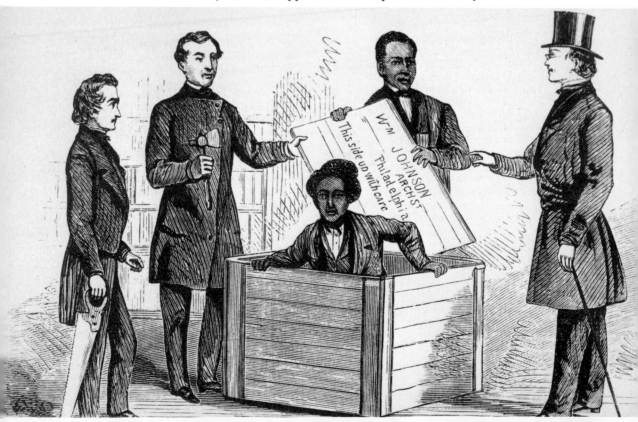

Abolitionist
James G. Birney

Harriet Beecher Stowe,
author of *Uncle Tom's Cabin*

Antislavery senator
Charles Sumner

Antislavery poet
John Greenleaf Whittier

北亞墨利加人物　ペルリ像

Chapter 9

Advancing the Ideas
of a Lifetime

Fillmore is best remembered for those things he least wanted to do as president. However, he was quite successful during his short presidency in advancing some of the causes he had always cared about. His enthusiasm for the development of commerce was reflected in his desire to open up trade with Japan. At the time Fillmore became president, there was only one Japanese port, Nagasaki, open to foreign ships. Even that port dealt only with the Dutch. There were also many reports of American sailors who had been mistreated after they were forced to land on Japanese soil in emergencies.

Fillmore commissioned Commodore Matthew Perry to approach Japanese leaders and negotiate a treaty. In 1853, Perry sailed a small fleet boldly into the Bay of Yeddo. He ignored an order by Japanese officials to sail for Nagasaki. Instead, he stayed where he was, allowing the Japanese to board his ship and examine its guns. He met with representatives of the emperor and explained why he had come.

Opposite page: Commodore Perry,
as painted by a Japanese artist

Matthew Perry, the man who "opened Japan"

Eventually, Perry was able to negotiate the Treaty of Peace and Amity (the "Perry Treaty"). This agreement opened up Japanese ports to U.S. ships and also guaranteed humane treatment of American seamen on Japanese soil. Though the treaty was not signed until 1854, it was Fillmore who had made Perry's trip possible. The treaty and subsequent trade brought Japan from isolation into world affairs and dramatically affected the course of history.

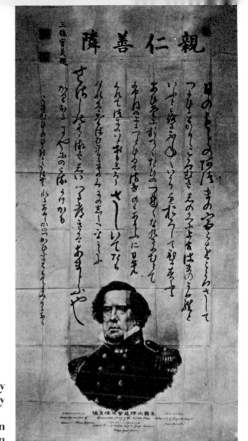

Right: A Japanese copy of the Perry Treaty

Below: Perry's expedition landing in Japan

Fillmore had always been interested in developing the nation's railways. While in Congress, he had helped arrange the first federal land grants to railroads. As president, he called for a transcontinental railroad. Again, his vision ran ahead of the times; it would be a later presidency that saw the railroad built. Nevertheless, railroad lines were being laid everywhere, thanks to the land grants. Fillmore traveled widely to celebrate the opening of new lines.

Fillmore also tried to arrange an agreement for building a canal in Nicaragua across Central America. This would give the United States an edge in the race with Britain for trade across the Pacific. However, clashes with Great Britain and with local Nicaraguan leaders finally made that project impossible. Fillmore also supported attempts to build a railroad line across the Tehuantepec peninsula in Mexico to speed up the transfer of goods across the Pacific. In Mexico, however, he encountered a great deal of hostility left over from the Mexican War. In addition, the private citizens trying to raise money for the project fought among themselves. Finally that project, too, had to be abandoned. But the idea of a gateway for ships or trains through Central America had come to life in American minds. It would be realized, as would the transcontinental railroad, another day.

Many of Fillmore's proposals came into effect only under later presidents: a court of claims, where citizens had some recourse against the federal government for debts it owed them; a Department of Agriculture; and a national archive to house the nation's records.

Governor Brigham Young of the Utah Territory

For the most part, Fillmore appointed people to government jobs on the basis of their ability and not simply for political loyalty. Except for the cabinet, he replaced few of Taylor's appointees. With one exception, he did not even replace the people Weed had put into federal jobs.

His most controversial appointment was surely that of Mormon church leader Brigham Young to be territorial governor of Utah. The choice was a logical one, since Young was the actual leader of the Mormons. Nevertheless, Young quickly got into trouble with federal authorities. They accused him of flaunting the law, particularly because he openly promoted polygamy, or multiple marriage. Eventually, it took a military expedition to get Young out of the governorship.

Fillmore took an active interest in foreign affairs. His attitude was simple and straightforward, as shown in his first annual message to Congress in 1850:

> We should act towards other nations as we wish them to act towards us, and justice and conscience should form the rules of conduct between governments, instead of mere power and self-interest, or the desire for aggrandizement. To maintain a strict neutrality in foreign wars, to cultivate friendly relations, to reciprocate every noble and generous act, and to perform punctually and scrupulously every Treaty obligation — these are the duties which we owe to other States.

Fillmore was never in favor of expanding American borders by force. When a group of American adventurers invaded Cuba in 1851, they were caught and immediately executed. Despite protests that the U.S. should take advantage of the incident to gain control of Cuba, Fillmore stood firm. When another private American ship threatened to enter Cuba's waters, Fillmore had it forcibly restrained in an American port. He refused to aid any attempt to take Cuba by force, particularly because it was viewed by many Americans as a source of slaves. Also, some southerners were hoping to make it a sixteenth slave state.

Fillmore was a hard-working president. He generally stayed at his desk until 10:30 P.M. and rarely left Washington. However, he rested on Sundays and enjoyed carriage rides around the city in his rare free moments. He was known for his courtly dignity at social functions, especially the many receptions and dinners held at the White House. Though Abigail's health had improved and she had joined him in Washington, it was really his daughter, Mary Abigail, who acted as White House hostess. Mary Abigail was a fluent speaker of French and Spanish, an accomplished musician, and a gracious hostess. Fillmore's son, Millard Powers, also joined him during the White House years. He served as the president's secretary and personal representative in sensitive or confidential matters.

Fillmore, an avid reader, had been appalled when he discovered that the White House had no library. He requested and received funds from Congress to establish one; the library became Abigail's retreat and the social center of the family. Among the lasting friendships Fillmore made during his years in the presidency was that of the American writer Washington Irving.

Fillmore had not expected to become president and had no real desire for a second term. As early as November 1850, he wrote to a friend: "I believe I am holding the last office that I shall ever hold, and have no desire to prolong it one minute beyond the Constitutional time." Even if he had wanted to run again, he knew that his role in the compromise had cost him his most loyal supporters.

Yet he was not willing to see the Whig party collapse or to give up control of it to William Seward, who was closely allied with Thurlow Weed. Neither did he want to be known as a "lame duck" president—one who need not be respected because he would soon be out of power. He kept his intentions to himself and encouraged Daniel Webster to seek the Whig nomination. On the side, he let it be known that he would not seek the nomination but would accept it if it were offered. Seward in the meantime was gathering support for his candidate, General Winfield Scott, a Mexican War hero.

Above: A magnificent wine-colored carriage, presented by the citizens of New York to Mrs. Millard Fillmore when she was First Lady. With silver trim and blue silken seat coverings, its appearance created quite a stir.

Right: American writer Washington Irving, a good friend of Millard Fillmore's

Opposite page: Mary Abigail Fillmore, Millard's daughter, who acted as White House hostess while Fillmore was president

Whig candidate Winfield Scott

Webster's campaign floundered from the beginning. Like Fillmore, he had been damaged by his support of the Compromise of 1850. When the Whig convention opened in June 1852, about half the delegates were committed to Fillmore, half to Scott, and only a handful to Webster. The convention quickly adopted a platform supporting the compromise. Satisfied with that move, Fillmore asked that his name be withdrawn as a nominee. His supporters refused, and the battle for the nomination began. As ballot after ballot was cast, Fillmore's delegates could not agree to support Webster, nor did Webster release his delegates to support Fillmore until it was too late. At last, on the fifty-third ballot, the nomination went to Winfield Scott. His candidacy marked the end of the Whig party. In the election he carried only four states, and the Democrats, under Franklin Pierce, regained the presidency.

President Franklin Pierce

Inauguration day must have been an ordeal for Pierce, whose son had been killed in a railway accident on his way to Washington to see the ceremony. Nevertheless, he went through with the ceremony and his speech encouraged Fillmore. He strongly endorsed the Compromise of 1850 and praised the "wise counsels" of those who had carried the nation through its crisis.

But Pierce's was not the only tragedy of the inauguration. Abigail Fillmore, who sat through the ceremony outdoors on a chilly, windy March day, contracted a severe cold that turned into pneumonia. She died March 30, and the Fillmore family returned to Buffalo to bury her the next day. Millard Fillmore prepared for a lonely retirement.

"The American Twins, or North and South" — a British cartoon
published in 1856, during the Kansas-Nebraska controversy

Chapter 10

The Know-Nothing
Campaign of 1856

After Fillmore's return to Buffalo, two major issues were dominating the American political scene. One was a proposal by Senator Stephen Douglas known as the Kansas-Nebraska Act. It would allow the new territories of Kansas and Nebraska to choose whether to permit slavery. Passed in March of 1854, it overturned the Missouri Compromise of 1820. That act had guaranteed that all territory north of the 36°30′ line (which included Kansas and Nebraska) would prohibit slavery.

The other issue was the growing nativist movement, which came together as the American party. It was more often called the Know-Nothing party. That name came from the secrecy associated with membership. When asked about the group's practices and goals, members would respond, "I know nothing." This group was extremely anti-Catholic. Although it did not oppose immigration, it favored restrictions on the rights of immigrants to vote and to hold public office. One of its proposals was a twenty-one-year residency requirement for citizenship.

An 1855 engraving of a lovely spot in Kansas

Just why or how Fillmore was drawn back into public life is unclear. In the early spring of 1854, he toured a number of states in the southeast and took a trip from Chicago to Saint Louis on some newly opened railroad lines. All along his route, he met with Whig leaders and spoke publicly. He did not, however, comment about either the Kansas-Nebraska Act or the nativist movement. He did not appear to be campaigning for public office.

Yet he must have been restless. He had not returned to his former profession, because he felt it improper for a former president to practice law. His time was thus consumed entirely by whatever private amusements were available and by the civic projects in which he was constantly involved. Then, in July of 1854, his daughter Mary Abigail died at age twenty-two, after an illness of only a few hours. Fillmore was devastated. Still mourning the

A boardinghouse for immigrants in nineteenth-century New York City

death of his wife, he had now lost the daughter who was his pride and comfort. It may have been to escape his grief that he thrust himself back into public life.

Whatever motivated him, he had become actively involved with the nativist movement by the winter of 1854 to 1855. In those days, before radio or television or even national newspapers, public figures who wanted their ideas known often wrote letters that they intended to be shared. In January 1855, Fillmore wrote such a letter to his friend Isaac Newton, a Know-Nothing party leader. Fillmore stated that he regretted the "corrupting influence" that the contests for immigrants' votes had on elections. He said that he thought the United States should welcome European immigrants, but that they should not be allowed to hold public office.

The Know-Nothings never became a major political party. Their doctrines were offensive to hundreds of thousands of recent immigrants who had become citizens and could vote. The party was equally offensive to the many native-born Americans who valued democratic government. Furthermore, the party's tremendous bias against Catholics was a sore point in a country that had clearly separated church and state.

Yet Fillmore agreed to become the Know-Nothing candidate for president in 1856. His reasons for doing so are not entirely clear. It was true that by this time the Whig party was almost gone, and Fillmore was cut off from what little of it was left because of his wars with Thurlow Weed. The Know-Nothings had done well in the 1854 elections in New York. To some Whigs, including Fillmore, saving the Union was more important than abolishing slavery. The Know-Nothings looked like the one group that could present a candidate who would keep the country united.

It is also possible that Fillmore believed in some of the nativist principles of the Know-Nothings. He had resented the Catholic immigrants in New York City ever since his humiliating loss in the 1844 race for governor. He sincerely believed their votes were likely to be influenced by the orders of the Pope—a foreign ruler. He feared that they had not been in this country long enough to understand its structure and appreciate its principles. Finally, he was alarmed at the growing system of private, religious schools they were creating. A firm supporter of public education, he feared that support for these private schools would eventually mean neglect of the public schools.

Above: An 1856 cartoon making fun of the Know-Nothings
Below: A British cartoon showing Know-Nothings in New Orleans's Mardi Gras parade

The 1856 Know-Nothing party convention—Fillmore was the presidential candidate and Andrew Jackson Donelson, former president Jackson's nephew, was the vice-presidential candidate.

Whatever his reasons, Fillmore joined the secret nativist society called the Order of the Star Spangled Banner. He announced his interest in the presidency and left for a year of travel in Europe while others prepared the way for his 1856 campaign. Although primarily a tourist during this period, he called on European leaders and surprised them with his elegant manners. In those days, many Europeans still thought that all Americans were rough country people cutting their way through forests with hatchets and living off what they could find!

Though he was refined, however, Fillmore was still a plain-spoken and humble man. In England, he was offered an honorary degree from Oxford University. This was a great honor, but he turned it down. The degree would have been printed in Latin, and Fillmore did not know that language. He said, "No man should . . . accept a degree he cannot read."

By the time Fillmore returned from Europe and received the Know-Nothing nomination for president, the party was already in trouble. It had not been able to capture all the Whig support it had hoped. Fillmore had brought in many of the "National" Whigs—Whigs who were committed above all to preserving the Union. However, Seward and Weed were organizing the "Conscience" Whigs—those who were committed to abolition even if it meant civil disobedience—into one party with the Republicans.

The remainder of the Whig party endorsed Fillmore as its candidate for president, but their support was not enough. Afraid that a split in what used to be the Whig vote would ensure a Republican victory, many of Fillmore's once-loyal supporters deserted him in favor of the Democratic candidate, James Buchanan. In the end, Buchanan won the 1856 election easily. Fillmore took only the state of Maryland. It was a humiliating defeat and the end of his political career.

Chapter 11

First Citizen of Buffalo

From the time he left the presidency in 1853 to the day of his death, Fillmore never returned to Washington. His decision was a matter of principle. He wished to play the role of "elder statesman" and felt that active involvement in politics was not appropriate for one in that role. After the 1856 Know-Nothing campaign, he lived quietly as the "First Citizen of Buffalo." He married a wealthy widow, Mrs. Caroline McIntosh, in 1858. They moved to a beautiful home on Niagara Square and lived in grand style, entertaining frequently. Fillmore, who did not have the generous pension of later presidents, was relieved of his money worries. Though he managed his new wife's money and took a fee for doing so, he left it all in her name.

Those who knew Fillmore described him as reserved, modest, and deliberate. His concern for others was such that he once took a dangerous ride in a cable car over the Niagara River, just so that a woman who insisted on going would not have to be alone. In Buffalo, he read to the workers in the local shoe factory, founded and served as president of the Buffalo General Hospital, and continued to promote public libraries and public education.

Opposite page: Millard Fillmore, photographed by Mathew Brady

Caroline
Carmichael
McIntosh
Fillmore,
Millard's
second wife

When the Civil War broke out in 1861, Fillmore, who
had so long opposed that war, nevertheless strongly supported the Union effort. Too old for active service, he
organized the "Union Continentals," a company of older
men who stood ready to act in the event of a local
emergency. The Continentals also promoted the war
effort, helped raise funds, and made appearances at public
functions. With $500 of his own money, Fillmore started a
fund to support the families of volunteers.

In spite of all his efforts on behalf of the Union forces,
however, he was bitterly attacked by many because he criticized the Republican party. (Republican Abraham Lincoln
was president then.) Fillmore said openly that the Republicans could and should have avoided the war. Although
often accused of treason, he refused to be silent. He had

Millard Fillmore,
born January 7, 1800,
died March 8, 1874

shown at his first apprenticeship that he would not be bullied. At sixty-four, he had lost none of that resolve.

Fillmore was active and healthy until virtually the hour of his death, bragging that he had taken "but one dose of medicine" in thirty years and that he had never been sick an hour while chairman of the Ways and Means Committee or president of the United States. In February 1874, however, he suffered a stroke that left him disabled; in March, a second stroke killed him.

President Ulysses S. Grant and other officials attended his funeral, but his death caused little sorrow outside of Buffalo. Although he had done what he thought was right throughout his public life, he was remembered not as a statesman but as a bigot and a traitor. In actual fact, he had destroyed his own career for what he saw as the preservation of the Union, and the Union had survived.

Chronology of American History

(Shaded area covers events in Millard Fillmore's lifetime.)

About A.D. 982—Eric the Red, born in Norway, reaches Greenland in one of the first European voyages to North America.

About 1000—Leif Ericson (Eric the Red's son) leads what is thought to be the first European expedition to mainland North America; Leif probably lands in Canada.

1492—Christopher Columbus, seeking a sea route from Spain to the Far East, discovers the New World.

1497—John Cabot reaches Canada in the first English voyage to North America.

1513—Ponce de Léon explores Florida in search of the fabled Fountain of Youth.

1519-1521—Hernando Cortés of Spain conquers Mexico.

1534—French explorers led by Jacques Cartier enter the Gulf of St. Lawrence in Canada.

1540—Spanish explorer Francisco Coronado begins exploring the American Southwest, seeking the riches of the mythical Seven Cities of Cibola.

1565—St. Augustine, Florida, the first permanent European town in what is now the United States, is founded by the Spanish.

1607—Jamestown, Virginia, is founded, the first permanent English town in the present-day U.S.

1608—Frenchman Samuel de Champlain founds the village of Quebec, Canada.

1609—Henry Hudson explores the eastern coast of present-day U.S. for the Netherlands; the Dutch then claim parts of New York, New Jersey, Delaware, and Connecticut and name the area New Netherland.

1619—The English colonies' first shipment of black slaves arrives in Jamestown.

1620—English Pilgrims found Massachusetts's first permanent town at Plymouth.

1621—Massachusetts Pilgrims and Indians hold the famous first Thanksgiving feast in colonial America.

1623—Colonization of New Hampshire is begun by the English.

1624—Colonization of present-day New York State is begun by the Dutch at Fort Orange (Albany).

1625—The Dutch start building New Amsterdam (now New York City).

1630—The town of Boston, Massachusetts, is founded by the English Puritans.

1633—Colonization of Connecticut is begun by the English.

1634—Colonization of Maryland is begun by the English.

1636—Harvard, the colonies' first college, is founded in Massachusetts. Rhode Island colonization begins when Englishman Roger Williams founds Providence.

1638—Delaware colonization begins as Swedes build Fort Christina at present-day Wilmington.

1640—Stephen Daye of Cambridge, Massachusetts prints *The Bay Psalm Book*, the first English-language book published in what is now the U.S.

1643—Swedish settlers begin colonizing Pennsylvania.

About 1650—North Carolina is colonized by Virginia settlers.

1660—New Jersey colonization is begun by the Dutch at present-day Jersey City.

1670—South Carolina colonization is begun by the English near Charleston.

1673—Jacques Marquette and Louis Jolliet explore the upper Mississippi River for France.

1682—Philadelphia, Pennsylvania, is settled. La Salle explores Mississippi River all the way to its mouth in Louisiana and claims the whole Mississippi Valley for France.

1693—College of William and Mary is founded in Williamsburg, Virginia.

1700—Colonial population is about 250,000.

1703—Benjamin Franklin is born in Boston.

1732—George Washington, first president of the U.S., is born in Westmoreland County, Virginia.

1733—James Oglethorpe founds Savannah, Georgia; Georgia is established as the thirteenth colony.

1735—John Adams, second president of the U.S., is born in Braintree, Massachusetts.

1737—William Byrd founds Richmond, Virginia.

1738—British troops are sent to Georgia over border dispute with Spain.

1739—Black insurrection takes place in South Carolina.

1740—English Parliament passes act allowing naturalization of immigrants to American colonies after seven-year residence.

1743—Thomas Jefferson is born in Albemarle County, Virginia. Benjamin Franklin retires at age thirty-seven to devote himself to scientific inquiries and public service.

1744—King George's War begins; France joins war effort against England.

1745—During King George's War, France raids settlements in Maine and New York.

1747—Classes begin at Princeton College in New Jersey.

1748—The Treaty of Aix-la-Chapelle concludes King George's War.

1749—Parliament legally recognizes slavery in colonies and the inauguration of the plantation system in the South. George Washington becomes the surveyor for Culpepper County in Virginia.

1750—Thomas Walker passes through and names Cumberland Gap on his way toward Kentucky region. Colonial population is about 1,200,000.

1751—James Madison, fourth president of the U.S., is born in Port Conway, Virginia. English Parliament passes Currency Act, banning New England colonies from issuing paper money. George Washington travels to Barbados.

1752—Pennsylvania Hospital, the first general hospital in the colonies, is founded in Philadelphia. Benjamin Franklin uses a kite in a thunderstorm to demonstrate that lightning is a form of electricity.

1753—George Washington delivers command that the French withdraw from the Ohio River Valley; French disregard the demand. Colonial population is about 1,328,000.

1754—French and Indian War begins (extends to Europe as the Seven Years' War). Washington surrenders at Fort Necessity.

1755—French and Indians ambush Braddock. Washington becomes commander of Virginia troops.

1756—England declares war on France.

1758—James Monroe, fifth president of the U.S., is born in Westmoreland County, Virginia.

1759—Cherokee Indian war begins in southern colonies; hostilities extend to 1761. George Washington marries Martha Dandridge Custis.

1760—George III becomes king of England. Colonial population is about 1,600,000.

1762—England declares war on Spain.

1763—Treaty of Paris concludes the French and Indian War and the Seven Years' War. England gains Canada and most other French lands east of the Mississippi River.

1764—British pass the Sugar Act to gain tax money from the colonists. The issue of taxation without representation is first introduced in Boston. John Adams marries Abigail Smith.

1765—Stamp Act goes into effect in the colonies. Business virtually stops as almost all colonists refuse to use the stamps.

1766—British repeal the Stamp Act.

1767—John Quincy Adams, sixth president of the U.S. and son of second president John Adams, is born in Braintree, Massachusetts. Andrew Jackson, seventh president of the U.S., is born in Waxhaw settlement, South Carolina.

1769—Daniel Boone sights the Kentucky Territory.

1770—In the Boston Massacre, British soldiers kill five colonists and injure six. Townshend Acts are repealed, thus eliminating all duties on imports to the colonies except tea.

1771—Benjamin Franklin begins his autobiography, a work that he will never complete. The North Carolina assembly passes the "Bloody Act," which makes rioters guilty of treason.

1772—Samuel Adams rouses colonists to consider British threats to self-government.

1773—English Parliament passes the Tea Act. Colonists dressed as Mohawk Indians board British tea ships and toss 342 casks of tea into the water in what becomes known as the Boston Tea Party. William Henry Harrison is born in Charles City County, Virginia.

1774—British close the port of Boston to punish the city for the Boston Tea Party. First Continental Congress convenes in Philadelphia.

1775—American Revolution begins with battles of Lexington and Concord, Massachusetts. Second Continental Congress opens in Philadelphia. George Washington becomes commander-in-chief of the Continental army.

1776—Declaration of Independence is adopted on July 4.

1777—Congress adopts the American flag with thirteen stars and thirteen stripes. John Adams is sent to France to negotiate peace treaty.

1778—France declares war against Great Britain and becomes U.S. ally.

1779—British surrender to Americans at Vincennes. Thomas Jefferson is elected governor of Virginia. James Madison is elected to the Continental Congress.

1780—Benedict Arnold, first American traitor, defects to the British.

1781—Articles of Confederation go into effect. Cornwallis surrenders to George Washington at Yorktown, ending the American Revolution.

1782—American commissioners, including John Adams, sign peace treaty with British in Paris. Thomas Jefferson's wife, Martha, dies. Martin Van Buren is born in Kinderhook, New York.

1784—Zachary Taylor is born near Barboursville, Virginia.

1785—Congress adopts the dollar as the unit of currency. John Adams is made minister to Great Britain. Thomas Jefferson is appointed minister to France.

1786—Shays's Rebellion begins in Massachusetts.

1787—Constitutional Convention assembles in Philadelphia, with George Washington presiding; U.S. Constitution is adopted. Delaware, New Jersey, and Pennsylvania become states.

1788—Virginia, South Carolina, New York, Connecticut, New Hampshire, Maryland, and Massachusetts become states. U.S. Constitution is ratified. New York City is declared U.S. capital.

1789—Presidential electors elect George Washington and John Adams as first president and vice-president. Thomas Jefferson is appointed secretary of state. North Carolina becomes a state. French Revolution begins.

1790—Supreme Court meets for the first time. Rhode Island becomes a state. First national census in the U.S. counts 3,929,214 persons. John Tyler is born in Charles City County, Virginia.

1791—Vermont enters the Union. U.S. Bill of Rights, the first ten amendments to the Constitution, goes into effect. District of Columbia is established. James Buchanan is born in Stony Batter, Pennsylvania.

1792—Thomas Paine publishes *The Rights of Man.* Kentucky becomes a state. Two political parties are formed in the U.S., Federalist and Republican. Washington is elected to a second term, with Adams as vice-president.

1793—War between France and Britain begins; U.S. declares neutrality. Eli Whitney invents the cotton gin; cotton production and slave labor increase in the South.

1794—Eleventh Amendment to the Constitution is passed, limiting federal courts' power. "Whiskey Rebellion" in Pennsylvania protests federal whiskey tax. James Madison marries Dolley Payne Todd.

1795—George Washington signs the Jay Treaty with Great Britain. Treaty of San Lorenzo, between U.S. and Spain, settles Florida boundary and gives U.S. right to navigate the Mississippi. James Polk is born near Pineville, North Carolina.

1796—Tennessee enters the Union. Washington gives his Farewell Address, refusing a third presidential term. John Adams is elected president and Thomas Jefferson vice-president.

1797—Adams recommends defense measures against possible war with France. Napoleon Bonaparte and his army march against Austrians in Italy. U.S. population is about 4,900,000.

1798—Washington is named commander-in-chief of the U.S. Army. Department of the Navy is created. Alien and Sedition Acts are passed. Napoleon's troops invade Egypt and Switzerland.

1799—George Washington dies at Mount Vernon, New York. James Monroe is elected governor of Virginia. French Revolution ends. Napoleon becomes ruler of France.

1800—Thomas Jefferson and Aaron Burr tie for president. U.S. capital is moved from Philadelphia to Washington, D.C. The White House is built as presidents' home. Spain returns Louisiana to France. Millard Fillmore is born in Locke, New York.

1801—After thirty-six ballots, House of Representatives elects Thomas Jefferson president, making Burr vice-president. James Madison is named secretary of state.

1802—Congress abolishes excise taxes. U.S. Military Academy is founded at West Point, New York.

1803—Ohio enters the Union. Louisiana Purchase treaty is signed with France, greatly expanding U.S. territory.

1804—Twelfth Amendment to the Constitution rules that president and vice-president be elected separately. Alexander Hamilton is killed by Vice-President Aaron Burr in a duel. Orleans Territory is established. Napoleon crowns himself emperor of France. Franklin Pierce is born in Hillsborough Lower Village, New Hampshire.

1805—Thomas Jefferson begins his second term as president. Lewis and Clark expedition reaches the Pacific Ocean.

1806—Coinage of silver dollars is stopped; resumes in 1836.

1807—Aaron Burr is acquitted in treason trial. Embargo Act closes U.S. ports to trade.

1808—James Madison is elected president. Congress outlaws importing slaves from Africa. Andrew Johnson is born in Raleigh, North Carolina.

1809—Abraham Lincoln is born near Hodgenville, Kentucky.

1810—U.S. population is 7,240,000.

1811—William Henry Harrison defeats Indians at Tippecanoe. Monroe is named secretary of state.

1812—Louisiana becomes a state. U.S. declares war on Britain (War of 1812). James Madison is reelected president. Napoleon invades Russia.

1813—British forces take Fort Niagara and Buffalo, New York.

1814—Francis Scott Key writes "The Star-Spangled Banner." British troops burn much of Washington, D.C., including the White House. Treaty of Ghent ends War of 1812. James Monroe becomes secretary of war.

1815—Napoleon meets his final defeat at Battle of Waterloo.

1816—James Monroe is elected president. Indiana becomes a state.

1817—Mississippi becomes a state. Construction on Erie Canal begins.

1818—Illinois enters the Union. The present thirteen-stripe flag is adopted. Border between U.S. and Canada is agreed upon.

1819—Alabama becomes a state. U.S. purchases Florida from Spain. Thomas Jefferson establishes the University of Virginia.

1820—James Monroe is reelected. In the Missouri Compromise, Maine enters the Union as a free (non-slave) state.

1821 — Missouri enters the Union as a slave state. Santa Fe Trail opens the American Southwest. Mexico declares independence from Spain. Napoleon Bonaparte dies.

1822 — U.S. recognizes Mexico and Colombia. Liberia in Africa is founded as a home for freed slaves. Ulysses S. Grant is born in Point Pleasant, Ohio. Rutherford B. Hayes is born in Delaware, Ohio.

1823 — Monroe Doctrine closes North and South America to European colonizing or invasion.

1824 — House of Representatives elects John Quincy Adams president when none of the four candidates wins a majority in national election. Mexico becomes a republic.

1825 — Erie Canal is opened. U.S. population is 11,300,000.

1826 — Thomas Jefferson and John Adams both die on July 4, the fiftieth anniversary of the Declaration of Independence.

1828 — Andrew Jackson is elected president. Tariff of Abominations is passed, cutting imports.

1829 — James Madison attends Virginia's constitutional convention. Slavery is abolished in Mexico. Chester A. Arthur is born in Fairfield, Vermont.

1830 — Indian Removal Act to resettle Indians west of the Mississippi is approved.

1831 — James Monroe dies in New York City. James A. Garfield is born in Orange, Ohio. Cyrus McCormick develops his reaper.

1832 — Andrew Jackson, nominated by the new Democratic Party, is reelected president.

1833 — Britain abolishes slavery in its colonies. Benjamin Harrison is born in North Bend, Ohio.

1835 — Federal government becomes debt-free for the first time.

1836 — Martin Van Buren becomes president. Texas wins independence from Mexico. Arkansas joins the Union. James Madison dies at Montpelier, Virginia.

1837 — Michigan enters the Union. U.S. population is 15,900,000. Grover Cleveland is born in Caldwell, New Jersey.

1840 — William Henry Harrison is elected president.

1841 — President Harrison dies in Washington, D.C., one month after inauguration. Vice-President John Tyler succeeds him.

1843 — William McKinley is born in Niles, Ohio.

1844 — James Knox Polk is elected president. Samuel Morse sends first telegraphic message.

1845 — Texas and Florida become states. Potato famine in Ireland causes massive emigration from Ireland to U.S. Andrew Jackson dies near Nashville, Tennessee.

1846 — Iowa enters the Union. War with Mexico begins.

1847 — U.S. captures Mexico City.

1848 — John Quincy Adams dies in Washington, D.C. Zachary Taylor becomes president. Treaty of Guadalupe Hidalgo ends Mexico-U.S. war. Wisconsin becomes a state.

1849 — James Polk dies in Nashville, Tennessee.

1850 — President Taylor dies in Washington, D.C.; Vice-President Millard Fillmore succeeds him. California enters the Union, breaking tie between slave and free states.

1852 — Franklin Pierce is elected president.

1853 — Gadsden Purchase transfers Mexican territory to U.S.

1854 — "War for Bleeding Kansas" is fought between slave and free states.

1855 — Czar Nicholas I of Russia dies, succeeded by Alexander II.

1856 — James Buchanan is elected president. In Massacre of Potawatomi Creek, Kansas-slavers are murdered by free-staters. Woodrow Wilson is born in Staunton, Virginia.

1857 — William Howard Taft is born in Cincinnati, Ohio.

1858 — Minnesota enters the Union. Theodore Roosevelt is born in New York City.

1859 — Oregon becomes a state.

1860—Abraham Lincoln is elected president; South Carolina secedes from the Union in protest.

1861—Arkansas, Tennessee, North Carolina, and Virginia secede. Kansas enters the Union as a free state. Civil War begins.

1862—Union forces capture Fort Henry, Roanoke Island, Fort Donelson, Jacksonville, and New Orleans; Union armies are defeated at the battles of Bull Run and Fredericksburg. Martin Van Buren dies in Kinderhook, New York. John Tyler dies near Charles City, Virginia.

1863—Lincoln issues Emancipation Proclamation: all slaves held in rebelling territories are declared free. West Virginia becomes a state.

1864—Abraham Lincoln is reelected. Nevada becomes a state.

1865—Lincoln is assassinated in Washington, D.C., and succeeded by Andrew Johnson. U.S. Civil War ends on May 26. Thirteenth Amendment abolishes slavery. Warren G. Harding is born in Blooming Grove, Ohio.

1867—Nebraska becomes a state. U.S. buys Alaska from Russia for $7,200,000. Reconstruction Acts are passed.

1868—President Johnson is impeached for violating Tenure of Office Act, but is acquitted by Senate. Ulysses S. Grant is elected president. Fourteenth Amendment prohibits voting discrimination. James Buchanan dies in Lancaster, Pennsylvania.

1869—Franklin Pierce dies in Concord, New Hampshire.

1870—Fifteenth Amendment gives blacks the right to vote.

1872—Grant is reelected over Horace Greeley. General Amnesty Act pardons ex-Confederates. Calvin Coolidge is born in Plymouth Notch, Vermont.

1874—Millard Fillmore dies in Buffalo, New York. Herbert Hoover is born in West Branch, Iowa.

1875—Andrew Johnson dies in Carter's Station, Tennessee.

1876—Colorado enters the Union. "Custer's last stand": he and his men are massacred by Sioux Indians at Little Big Horn, Montana.

1877—Rutherford B. Hayes is elected president as all disputed votes are awarded to him.

1880—James A. Garfield is elected president.

1881—President Garfield is assassinated and dies in Elberon, New Jersey. Vice-President Chester A. Arthur succeeds him.

1882—U.S. bans Chinese immigration. Franklin D. Roosevelt is born in Hyde Park, New York.

1884—Grover Cleveland is elected president. Harry S. Truman is born in Lamar, Missouri.

1885—Ulysses S. Grant dies in Mount McGregor, New York.

1886—Statue of Liberty is dedicated. Chester A. Arthur dies in New York City.

1888—Benjamin Harrison is elected president.

1889—North Dakota, South Dakota, Washington, and Montana become states.

1890—Dwight D. Eisenhower is born in Denison, Texas. Idaho and Wyoming become states.

1892—Grover Cleveland is elected president.

1893—Rutherford B. Hayes dies in Fremont, Ohio.

1896—William McKinley is elected president. Utah becomes a state.

1898—U.S. declares war on Spain over Cuba.

1900—McKinley is reelected. Boxer Rebellion against foreigners in China begins.

1901—McKinley is assassinated by anarchist Leon Czolgosz in Buffalo, New York; Theodore Roosevelt becomes president. Benjamin Harrison dies in Indianapolis, Indiana.

1902—U.S. acquires perpetual control over Panama Canal.

1903—Alaskan frontier is settled.

1904—Russian-Japanese War breaks out. Theodore Roosevelt wins presidential election.

1905—Treaty of Portsmouth signed, ending Russian-Japanese War.

1906—U.S. troops occupy Cuba.

1907—President Roosevelt bars all Japanese immigration. Oklahoma enters the Union.

1908—William Howard Taft becomes president. Grover Cleveland dies in Princeton, New Jersey. Lyndon B. Johnson is born near Stonewall, Texas.

1909—NAACP is founded under W.E.B. DuBois

1910—China abolishes slavery.

1911—Chinese Revolution begins. Ronald Reagan is born in Tampico, Illinois.

1912—Woodrow Wilson is elected president. Arizona and New Mexico become states.

1913—Federal income tax is introduced in U.S. through the Sixteenth Amendment. Richard Nixon is born in Yorba Linda, California. Gerald Ford is born in Omaha, Nebraska.

1914—World War I begins.

1915—British liner *Lusitania* is sunk by German submarine.

1916—Wilson is reelected president.

1917—U.S. breaks diplomatic relations with Germany. Czar Nicholas of Russia abdicates as revolution begins. U.S. declares war on Austria-Hungary. John F. Kennedy is born in Brookline, Massachusetts.

1918—Wilson proclaims "Fourteen Points" as war aims. On November 11, armistice is signed between Allies and Germany.

1919—Eighteenth Amendment prohibits sale and manufacture of intoxicating liquors. Wilson presides over first League of Nations; wins Nobel Peace Prize. Theodore Roosevelt dies in Oyster Bay, New York.

1920—Nineteenth Amendment (women's suffrage) is passed. Warren Harding is elected president.

1921—Adolf Hitler's stormtroopers begin to terrorize political opponents.

1922—Irish Free State is established. Soviet states form USSR. Benito Mussolini forms Fascist government in Italy.

1923—President Harding dies in San Francisco, California; he is succeeded by Vice-President Calvin Coolidge.

1924—Coolidge is elected president. Woodrow Wilson dies in Washington, D.C. James Carter is born in Plains, Georgia. George Bush is born in Milton, Massachusetts.

1925—Hitler reorganizes Nazi Party and publishes first volume of *Mein Kampf.*

1926—Fascist youth organizations founded in Germany and Italy. Republic of Lebanon proclaimed.

1927—Stalin becomes Soviet dictator. Economic conference in Geneva attended by fifty-two nations.

1928—Herbert Hoover is elected president. U.S. and many other nations sign Kellogg-Briand pacts to outlaw war.

1929—Stock prices in New York crash on "Black Thursday"; the Great Depression begins.

1930—Bank of U.S. and its many branches close (most significant bank failure of the year). William Howard Taft dies in Washington, D.C.

1931—Emigration from U.S. exceeds immigration for first time as Depression deepens.

1932—Franklin D. Roosevelt wins presidential election in a Democratic landslide.

1933—First concentration camps are erected in Germany. U.S. recognizes USSR and resumes trade. Twenty-First Amendment repeals prohibition. Calvin Coolidge dies in Northampton, Massachusetts.

1934—Severe dust storms hit Plains states. President Roosevelt passes U.S. Social Security Act.

1936—Roosevelt is reelected. Spanish Civil War begins. Hitler and Mussolini form Rome-Berlin Axis.

1937—Roosevelt signs Neutrality Act.

1938—Roosevelt sends appeal to Hitler and Mussolini to settle European problems amicably.

1939—Germany takes over Czechoslovakia and invades Poland, starting World War II.

1940—Roosevelt is reelected for a third term.

1941—Japan bombs Pearl Harbor, U.S. declares war on Japan. Germany and Italy declare war on U.S.; U.S. then declares war on them.

1942—Allies agree not to make separate peace treaties with the enemies. U.S. government transfers more than 100,000 Nisei (Japanese-Americans) from west coast to inland concentration camps.

1943—Allied bombings of Germany begin.

1944—Roosevelt is reelected for a fourth term. Allied forces invade Normandy on D-Day.

1945—President Franklin D. Roosevelt dies in Warm Springs, Georgia; Vice-President Harry S. Truman succeeds him. Mussolini is killed; Hitler commits suicide. Germany surrenders. U.S. drops atomic bomb on Hiroshima; Japan surrenders: end of World War II.

1946—U.N. General Assembly holds its first session in London. Peace conference of twenty-one nations is held in Paris.

1947—Peace treaties are signed in Paris. "Cold War" is in full swing.

1948—U.S. passes Marshall Plan Act, providing $17 billion in aid for Europe. U.S. recognizes new nation of Israel. India and Pakistan become free of British rule. Truman is elected president.

1949—Republic of Eire is proclaimed in Dublin. Russia blocks land route access from Western Germany to Berlin; airlift begins. U.S., France, and Britain agree to merge their zones of occupation in West Germany. Apartheid program begins in South Africa.

1950—Riots in Johannesburg, South Africa, against apartheid. North Korea invades South Korea. U.N. forces land in South Korea and recapture Seoul.

1951—Twenty-Second Amendment limits president to two terms.

1952—Dwight D. Eisenhower resigns as supreme commander in Europe and is elected president.

1953—Stalin dies; struggle for power in Russia follows. Rosenbergs are executed for espionage.

1954—U.S. and Japan sign mutual defense agreement.

1955—Blacks in Montgomery, Alabama, boycott segregated bus lines.

1956—Eisenhower is reelected president. Soviet troops march into Hungary.

1957—U.S. agrees to withdraw ground forces from Japan. Russia launches first satellite, *Sputnik.*

1958—European Common Market comes into being. Fidel Castro begins war against Batista government in Cuba.

1959—Alaska becomes the forty-ninth state. Hawaii becomes fiftieth state. Castro becomes premier of Cuba. De Gaulle is proclaimed president of the Fifth Republic of France.

1960—Historic debates between Senator John F. Kennedy and Vice-President Richard Nixon are televised. Kennedy is elected president. Brezhnev becomes president of USSR.

1961—Berlin Wall is constructed. Kennedy and Khrushchev confer in Vienna. In Bay of Pigs incident, Cubans trained by CIA attempt to overthrow Castro.

1962—U.S. military council is established in South Vietnam.

1963—Riots and beatings by police and whites mark civil rights demonstrations in Birmingham, Alabama; 30,000 troops are called out, Martin Luther King, Jr., is arrested. Freedom marchers descend on Washington, D.C., to demonstrate. President Kennedy is assassinated in Dallas, Texas; Vice-President Lyndon B. Johnson is sworn in as president.

1964—U.S. aircraft bomb North Vietnam. Johnson is elected president. Herbert Hoover dies in New York City.

1965—U.S. combat troops arrive in South Vietnam.

1966—Thousands protest U.S. policy in Vietnam. National Guard quells race riots in Chicago.

1967—Six-Day War between Israel and Arab nations.

1968—Martin Luther King, Jr., is assassinated in Memphis, Tennessee. Senator Robert Kennedy is assassinated in Los Angeles. Riots and police brutality take place at Democratic National Convention in Chicago. Richard Nixon is elected president. Czechoslovakia is invaded by Soviet troops.

1969—Dwight D. Eisenhower dies in Washington, D.C. Hundreds of thousands of people in several U.S. cities demonstrate against Vietnam War.

1970—Four Vietnam War protesters are killed by National Guardsmen at Kent State University in Ohio.

1971—Twenty-Sixth Amendment allows eighteen-year-olds to vote.

1972—Nixon visits Communist China; is reelected president in near-record landslide. Watergate affair begins when five men are arrested in the Watergate hotel complex in Washington, D.C. Nixon announces resignations of aides Haldeman, Ehrlichman, and Dean and Attorney General Kleindienst as a result of Watergate-related charges. Harry S. Truman dies in Kansas City, Missouri.

1973—Vice-President Spiro Agnew resigns; Gerald Ford is named vice-president. Vietnam peace treaty is formally approved after nineteen months of negotiations. Lyndon B. Johnson dies in San Antonio, Texas.

1974—As a result of Watergate cover-up, impeachment is considered; Nixon resigns and Ford becomes president. Ford pardons Nixon and grants limited amnesty to Vietnam War draft evaders and military deserters.

1975—U.S. civilians are evacuated from Saigon, South Vietnam, as Communist forces complete takeover of South Vietnam.

1976—U.S. celebrates its Bicentennial. James Earl Carter becomes president.

1977—Carter pardons most Vietnam draft evaders, numbering some 10,000.

1980—Ronald Reagan is elected president.

1981—President Reagan is shot in the chest in assassination attempt. Sandra Day O'Connor is appointed first woman justice of the Supreme Court.

1983—U.S. troops invade island of Grenada.

1984—Reagan is reelected president. Democratic candidate Walter Mondale's running mate, Geraldine Ferraro, is the first woman selected for vice-president by a major U.S. political party.

1985—Soviet Communist Party secretary Konstantin Chernenko dies; Mikhail Gorbachev succeeds him. U.S. and Soviet officials discuss arms control in Geneva. Reagan and Gorbachev hold summit conference in Geneva. Racial tensions accelerate in South Africa.

1986—Space shuttle *Challenger* explodes shortly after takeoff; crew of seven dies. U.S. bombs bases in Libya. Corazon Aquino defeats Ferdinand Marcos in Philippine presidential election.

1987—Iraqi missile rips the U.S. frigate *Stark* in the Persian Gulf, killing thirty-seven American sailors. Congress holds hearings to investigate sale of U.S. arms to Iran to finance Nicaraguan *contra* movement.

1988—President Reagan and Soviet leader Gorbachev sign INF treaty, eliminating intermediate nuclear forces. Severe drought sweeps the United States. George Bush is elected president.

1989—East Germany opens Berlin Wall, allowing citizens free exit. Communists lose control of governments in Poland, Romania, and Czechoslovakia. Chinese troops massacre over 1,000 pro-democracy student demonstrators in Beijing's Tiananmen Square.

1990—Iraq annexes Kuwait, provoking the threat of war. East and West Germany are reunited. The Cold War between the United States and the Soviet Union comes to a close. Several Soviet republics make moves toward independence.

1991—Backed by a coalition of members of the United Nations, U.S. troops drive Iraqis from Kuwait. Latvia, Lithuania, and Estonia withdraw from the USSR. The Soviet Union dissolves as its republics secede to form a Commonwealth of Independent States.

1992—U.N. forces fail to stop fighting in territories of former Yugoslavia. More than fifty people are killed and more than six hundred buildings burned in rioting in Los Angeles. U.S. unemployment reaches eight-year high. Hurricane Andrew devastates southern Florida and parts of Louisiana. International relief supplies and troops are sent to combat famine and violence in Somalia.

1993—U.S.-led forces use airplanes and missiles to attack military targets in Iraq. William Jefferson Clinton becomes the forty-second U.S. president.

1994—Richard M. Nixon dies in New York City.

Index

Page numbers in boldface type indicate illustrations.

About the Author

Jane Clark Casey was born in Arkansas in 1947. She attended school in Arkansas, Missouri, and Colorado before settling in Illinois. Ms. Casey has worked as a grocery checker, pickle packer, reporter, domestic, librarian, secretary, judicial clerk, teacher, and attorney, but she thinks of herself as primarily a humorist. Having published poetry, features, and law review articles, this is her first foray into biography. Ms. Casey lives in Chicago with her husband, Frank, and son, John, and practices law with the firm of Winston & Strawn.